Tips from the Top

EDITED BY

Clifford Pearson, Ken Yeang,
and Raghda AlHayali

Tips from the Top

Architects Share Their Advice for Success

PA PRESS

PRINCETON ARCHITECTURAL PRESS · NEW YORK

Contents

VALUES

ENGAGEMENT

PROCESS

PERSONAL DEVELOPMENT

DETERMINATION

Advice on Advice

Take it with a grain of salt. What's helpful to one person may be useless to another. And what's useless now may turn out to be invaluable in the future. As comedians say, timing is everything.

Gene Kohn often told the story of a meeting he had when he was trying to launch Kohn Pedersen Fox in the second half of the 1970s. One powerful businessman told him, "Your success will depend on what you say 'no' to, as much as what you agree to." Gene left the meeting frustrated. He was looking for clients and projects, not advice. And he was in no position to say "no" to anything. A few months later, he was offered a huge project in a country where he had done some work at a previous firm. He realized, though, that KPF would have to hire a large number of employees and spend a significant amount of money on travel and other expenses. From previous experience, he knew clients in that part of the world were often slow in paying and reimbursing expenses. Incurring a large debt before it had any other sources of income could sink KPF before it really got going. All of a sudden, that annoying piece of advice from a few months earlier had new resonance. KPF turned down the job. Shortly thereafter, the leader of the country in question was pushed out of power and the people behind the big project fled to other places. KPF had dodged a bullet.

This book compiles tips from a broad range of architects and design professionals from around the world. We have organized the advice in seven broad categories—Beginnings, Inspiration, Values, Engagement, Process, Personal Development, and Determination—but some tips could fit in multiple categories. A recurring theme of many of the tips is the need to break free of boundaries. It's good advice for using this book as well as for practicing architecture.

We hope this book appeals to a spectrum of readers—from those just exploring the idea of architecture as a career to students in architecture school and graduates moving their way into the profession. While tips often come from the top, it's smart to learn from those on either side of you or even those below you. Also look beyond architecture for inspiration, good ideas, and help. Films, books, articles on obscure topics, art exhibitions, overheard conversations, walks in the woods, demographic data sets, business trends, science fiction, and poetry may all influence your way of thinking about design if you keep your eyes open and your mind supple.

As you browse through this book, search not just for the names you know but for those you don't. Look for architects in faraway places, as well as those nearby. Go online and check out their work and their writings. Go beyond the short tips in this book and explore the ideas and projects these architects have developed over the years.

Treat this book as a snack box, a source of nourishing advice you can raid whenever you're hungry and need some help.

Sometimes you need to hear a piece of advice multiple times before it sinks in and starts to mean something. Trust is an essential element in this process, so try to develop networks of people whose judgment and expertise you respect. Don't abuse their generosity, but keep them informed of progress that you make over time. Successful people like to see their advice work and will often help make that happen. Take advantage of that.

Good luck!

A further note on advice: This book project was launched in 2020 right before the worldwide pandemic when a twenty-eight-year-old architect in the United Arab Emirates started asking more senior people for tips on success. She realized other young architects could probably benefit from such help too, so she came up with the title, *Tips from the Top*, and widened her search. One of the architects she contacted was Ken Yeang, who loved the idea so much he volunteered to help with the project. Ken then roped in Clifford Pearson to help pull things together. The young architect who got it all going was Raghda AlHayali and this is her first book. Great ideas don't always start at the top.

BEGINNINGS

Sebastian Schmaling
Partner, Johnsen Schmaling Architects, Milwaukee

→ Fit the scale of your ideas to the size of the project

The ambitions of young practitioners often collide with the practical constraints of their first commissions. Fueled by a mix of passion and impatience, fledgling designers often find themselves eager to manifest a grand architectural agenda from the outset, attempting to infuse every cherished idea into their maiden projects—even when the typically tight budgets and modest scales of those early commissions leave little room for creative exuberance. When an architect's boundless aspiration clashes with the inherent limitations of a project, the outcome can be disastrous. In the best case, the design may simply be unbuildable. In the worst, it may turn into a deeply confused, poorly executed building. Neither scenario is particularly conducive to the reputation of an emerging practice.

Recognizing that a single project is unlikely to encompass the entirety of one's architectural imagination, it is important to distill one or two specific goals that resonate profoundly with the designer. An intentional, strategic focus on a select few elements allows the architect to navigate around the many project constraints. This tailored approach transforms each commission into a deliberate stepping stone, where success is measured not by the grandiosity of a lofty concept but by the precise execution of relevant architectural objectives.

In essence, my advice is this: resist the allure of cramming an all-encompassing architectural agenda into your first commission; instead, strategically prioritize key elements. Through this measured approach, architects can lay the groundwork for a career marked by a mosaic of accomplishments, each project contributing to the realization of a broader architectural vision over time.

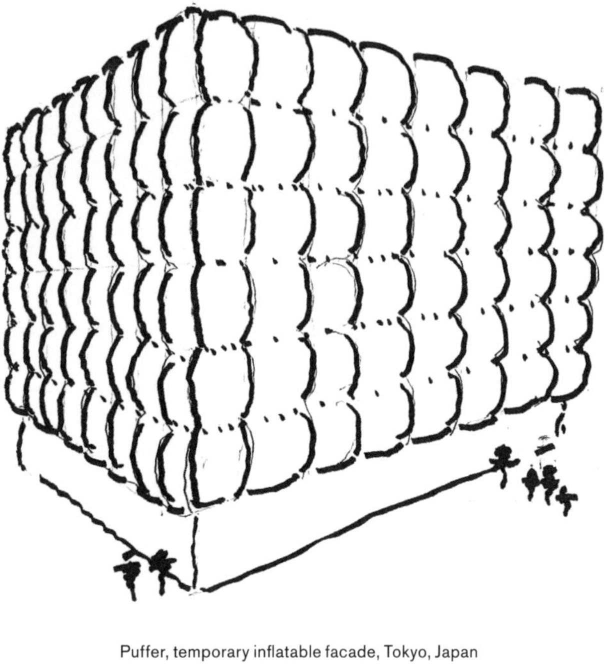

Puffer, temporary inflatable facade, Tokyo, Japan

Astrid Klein and Mark Dytham
Founders, Klein Dytham architecture (KDa), Tokyo

→ Be bold

Be bold with your designs!

At the Royal College of Art in London, we were always told by our wonderful tutor James Gowan at final project reviews: "You all talk too much!" He wanted us to pin up our work, and as we pushed in the last pin, collapse from creative exhaustion and "let the drawings say everything."

You cannot stand outside your building and say, "This is the concept. Look at this detail." The building has to speak for itself. It has to say everything and be understood by young and old.

We started our careers in Japan, where we couldn't speak the language, and most clients couldn't understand us. So our designs had to speak for themselves. They had to BE BOLD.

BE BOLD and let your ideas speak for themselves.

Hani Rashid

Co-founder and principal, Asymptote Architecture, New York

→ Take risks

While in architecture school in the 1980s, I found the discipline of architecture to be steeped in Postmodernism and, as it seemed at the time, a restrained philosophy and approach that relied far too heavily on the obvious. Yet, simultaneously, there was a sense in the air that the entire discipline of architecture was in a state of flux with dramatic changes looming, regardless of the stylistic flourishes of the time. With that sense of uncertainty while at school, I put all my efforts into researching, drawing, and making things that, at the time, seemed far from what was being peddled as architecture.

Once I graduated, I set out, perhaps naively, on my own as soon as possible and decided to enter an international competition to redesign the ancient Roman fortified town of Lanciano on the Adriatic coast of Italy. For ideas on master planning and architecture, I drew inspiration from unlikely sources, such as the seventeenth-century stories of Rabelais recounting the lives of the giants Gargantua and Pantagruel and the complex and vivid paintings of Futurist Carlo Carrà.

The only advice I can give with those memories in mind is to seek out opportunities that afford absolute risk-taking and then work at as extreme a level as possible to skirt the accepted and the obvious.

Mohammed Kamal Al Shurafa
Partner, Mimar Group, Dubai

→ Start off right

Young architects and fresh graduates should find a good place to start their professional career. The aim in the first years after school should be to continue their learning curve. An education at university is just a beginning: it opens the doors to learning the realities of architecture from within the profession.

Don't look at how much you're paid, but rather at how much you're learning. The more knowledge you acquire in your first years, the better architect you will become and the more responsibilities and income you will achieve. Save the best for last.

Viken Mahserejian
Director of architecture, MSCEB (Mohamed Salahuddin Architects & Engineers), Bahrain

→ Build a career

Think of architecture as a career, not just a job. Don't allow financial temptations or setbacks to divert you from it.

Try to work on every aspect of architecture in the first five to ten years of your career. Get experience doing concepts, presentations, renderings, details, construction drawings, material specifications, and construction-site visits.

Sharon Johnston and Mark Lee
Founding partners, Johnston Marklee, Los Angeles

→ Take it slow

Architecture is a slow art. It demands a lot of resources for its undertaking. When completed, it demands a lot of time for it to shape our lives and, in turn, demands a lot of attention to comprehend its efficacy.

Becoming an architect is an even slower process. It stipulates an exorbitant amount of time to attain the technical, professional, financial, and political prowess required to be an active contributor to the built environment.

At a moment when cultural tendencies overindulge in visual display, when there is more information available than attention, architecture could come across as an anachronistic practice, lagging behind other cultural practices that respond in quicker, louder, and more immediate ways.

But there is no reason to rush. Architecture does not need to compete with the speed of other cultural endeavors. Slowness is architecture's greatest asset. Let your architecture be slow.

Give the work a chance to mature; give it time to age like wine. Take advantage of architecture's intrinsic slowness.

Take your time to grow as an architect. There is no need to be on the fast track. There is no need to keep up with the latest microtrends. There is no need to adopt the model of unrelenting growth. It is okay to be on a slow burn.

Take your time to be very good, to be very serious, to establish your own pace in pursuing your architectural interests with tenacity and confidence. Take your time to produce quietly subversive work, which slowly reveals itself to those who give it their focus and attention.

Gregg Pasquarelli
Founding principal, SHoP Architects, New York

→ Make the first move

Here we are near the end of the first quarter of the twenty-first century and, amazingly, people still tend to think architecture is about heroic solo action—as if we all have to be Frank Lloyd Wright, Howard Roark, or Zaha Hadid all the time or nothing will get built.

The process of getting buildings built has always been intensely collaborative. Contractors, consultants, community reps, civic entities all play their roles. And then, of course, there is another C-word—the client, the generator of the demand for which we are being asked to supply a design solution. It's the client who usually owns or controls the site itself and is the source of the money necessary to rally and sustain the entire effort. We appreciate and admire the risks our clients take every day.

So, if there's no client, no money, no site, no program, then there's no architecture. Right? Not always. One of the biggest lessons I've learned—and one of the most successful strategies my firm, SHoP, has pursued since its earliest days—is that, when the stars align, architects can (and should!) make the first move.

You don't need to sit around waiting for your phone to ring or beep or buzz. Go out and get a project rolling yourself. First, make a lot of friends with people who are not architects: builders, bankers, politicians, people of all backgrounds and stripes. Then listen to them and learn how the world really works. You'll find that you are acquiring the knowledge, connections, and resources to flip the usual process on its head. You'll learn how to identify an architectural opportunity and then assemble the perfect team to meet that need—led by you and including, from your new contacts, the perfect client, the perfect collaborator, the perfect person with whom you can change the trajectory of how things are done. Just do it.

Arthur Andersson
President, Andersson/Wise, Austin, Texas

→ Lay a foundation for your work

First, immerse yourself in writings on architecture: history, theory, and biography. This will lay a foundation for your own thoughts and work. By reading the words of scholars, architects, and historians, you will develop a vocabulary of your own and a greater understanding of how to use it.

Second, learn to draw. Drawing is the architect's craft. Developing the ability to draw is essential to the exploration of your own concepts and to your success in communicating them. Drawings—by hand and digital—are the essential method by which an architect works with clients, colleagues, and construction teams to bring a building to fruition. Energy put into making fine and beautiful drawings will be seen in your work.

Finally, travel. Seek out places and buildings of cultural and architectural excellence. Look with humility and respect at the works of other designers and architects, past and present. Your own work will be improved by studying how other architects have addressed design challenges and opportunities. Successful architecture is closely tied to its place, both environmentally and culturally. Traveling with eyes and mind open will lead to a finer understanding of how buildings can shape culture.

Stone Creek Camp, Bigfork, Montana

Winka H. Dubbeldam
Founding partner, Archi-Tectonics, New York

→ Design what you believe in

Focus on your long-term goal. What kind of architect do you want to become? If you are aiming to follow your dream and start (eventually) your own office, then make sure that everything you do is focused on expanding that dream. This is harder than you might think. As one of my friends, screenwriter Nicholas Klein, wrote: "The courage to reach beyond your grasp will make you vulnerable, the vulnerability will give you wings, the wings will fly you beyond your dreams, where of course you may well be shot down. But if you live, which you likely will, you will without doubt be better than you were before."

We live in challenging times. My belief is that this offers an incredible opportunity for a new generation of architects. The Anthropocene has given us global warming, environmental change, pollution and waste, transition to new energy and resource economies, and the redistribution and reorganization of political and economic world powers; globalization of the construction and development industries; population growth, shrinkage, and migration; urban intensification and privatization of public-sector activities; and the transformation of cultural identities and social institutions. It is up to you to bring expansion of expertise and creativity in architecture to bear on these challenges. That means making sure to design what you believe in. Be research-oriented, rigorous, and proactive. Ask for what you want. Be courageous in what you design. And make sure to share your thoughts, designs, and research. You will need a team of expert collaborators to continually expand on digital design and robotic platforms, (bio)material research, and new manufacturing methods.

Most of all, have fun.

INSPIRATION

Scene of Unseen 09 by Dong Gong

Dong Gong
Founder and design principal,
Vector Architects, Beijing

→ Hold on to the basics

I have always been intrigued by the beauty of a tree. Its roots grasp the soil deep in the earth, striving hard for the strength to grow, while its canopy extends to the sky, swaying in the wind at ease. Such a state of tension is essential for an architect's efforts nowadays. Despite our dazzlingly fast-changing society and no matter how interactive your design sensibility might be, never lose hold of the basics. Be passionate about light, air, scale, materiality, atmosphere—all the eternal values that make architecture relevant to our bodies and minds.

Kongjian Yu
Founder, Turenscape, Beijing

→ Find the other way around

After practicing for more than two and a half decades, I have found one tip to be extremely useful: Think the opposite! As architects of buildings, cities, and landscapes, we are constantly looking for solutions to problems but are often stuck in a mindset shaped by conventional wisdom and established practice. The results are often dismally predictable. But if we take the other way around, then surprises always come.

What if, instead of forcing our vision of the city onto the land, we let nature shape the city's form? Then we have a totally different city whose inhabitants can benefit from nature's abundant services, such as storm-water management, beauty, and the provision of fresh air and food. What if we turn a building inside out, transform the inside walls into a living habitat, and let ferns flourish in the bedroom, instead of separating "inside" and "outside" with solid walls? Then we have suddenly created a healthier living space. What if we buck the convention that insists trees be planted only in well-drained ground and grow trees in water instead? Now we have a flood-adaptive and climate-resilient forest that provides a distinctive recreational space within the densely built urban environment—and a space that people can share with birds and other wildlife.

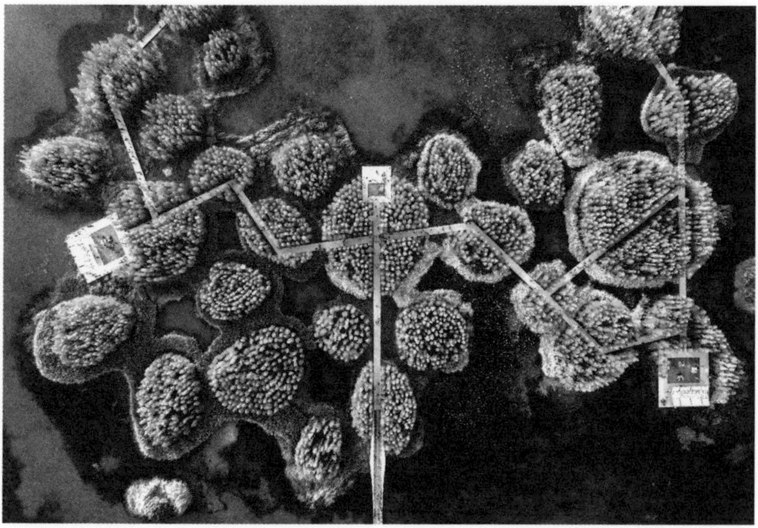

Fishtail Park, a floating forest for a resilient city, Nanchang City, China

Neil Denari
Principal, Neil M. Denari Architects, Los Angeles

→ Learn from other disciplines

Develop interests in related visual fields, such as film or painting. While both of those disciplines influence my thinking, the medium of graphic design figures most prominently in my practice. In addition to exploring how space can become graphic through material, color, and geometry, you can use graphic design techniques and sensibilities to present work in books, prints, and digital formats. You might study the work of people like Wim Crouwel, Irma Boom, and Josef Müller-Brockmann to learn how typography and grids work in the organization of graphic space for presentations.

Like a painter framing an artwork or a film director setting up a shot, you can use graphic design to provide a context for your work and how it will be read. Even in a lecture format, when spoken words and images (still and moving) carry the content along, you can treat the visual production as something between a discourse in film titles and an exploration of book design. Use text in specific ways to emphasize a point or further a mood or aesthetic. Whether you prefer left-justified sans-serif Modernism or centered serif Classicism (or anything in between), you should be precise about the forms and languages of graphic design that surround and support your architectural project. Experiment with styles. Seek out respected graphic designers to either design or critique this aspect of your work. This final touch means everything when you engage people with your ideas.

Roger Duffy

Partner emeritus, Skidmore, Owings & Merrill (SOM), New York

→ Imagine

Be someone who sees and feels in imaginative ways. Be open to the many forms of creativity. Seek outside the field of architecture for breathtaking works that make the hair stand up on the back of your neck. Keep your antenna alert; tune in these elevated, inventive revelations. Fully immerse yourself in the high notes of culture and nature.

Be a visionary. The mind creates a visual catalogue of collected "high note" impressions and remembrances that can be brought forward to create new project visions. Build consensus for your vision with your colleagues; they need to share in it. A compelling vision will always beckon audiences, so bring them into your vision as well. Your collective understanding will bring success.

Be prepared to embrace new opportunities as they arrive. Talent isn't enough; recognizing a good opportunity and embracing it moves talent to a higher level.

Be present. Offer a strong work ethic and be someone who solves problems. Communicate your thoughts as effectively as you can and collaborate generously. If challenged, be confident in your ability to figure things out.

Be engaged with the way things are. Recognize the reality of every situation; be humble as you address complexity. Seek a mentor who is truly great, who can teach, who builds confidence: someone who makes you feel like you can also be great.

Be yourself.

Iyad Alsaka
Partner, Office for Metropolitan Architecture (OMA), Rotterdam

→ Explore the edges

Innovation happens at intersections—the places where disciplines converge. So try to become a polymath, a multi-potential-ite. Develop expertise spanning different subject areas and draw on complex bodies of knowledge to solve complex conditions. Remember: new ideas emerge where fields overlap and knowledge is exchanged.

Kai-Uwe Bergmann
Partner, Bjarke Ingels Group (BIG), New York

→ See the world

In the words of Hans Christian Andersen, "To travel is to live." I think one of the greatest skills that we, as architects, acquire is drawing. Since this practice is universally the same from one country to the next, it offers a common language we can use to communicate anywhere in the world. By traveling we see the cities and the buildings designed by our ancestors. By traveling and working in other cultures and countries we expand our perspectives. This makes us better architects for life.

Imad Kayyali
VP of design and engineering, Controlled Environment Agriculture Design (CEAd), Burlington, Ontario

→ Dream big

Design with heart. Let nature inspire your canvas. Have the winds of your dream take your sail on wild adventures.

Luca Nicoletti
Senior architect, Bjarke Ingels Group (BIG), Copenhagen

→ Be curious and question everything

Curiosity energizes creativity, which comes from putting old ideas to the test. The past can be questioned, but today's architecture must evolve to provide the same quality and value that previous architecture produced. As architects, we should question every old and new idea to search for answers. After doing this, we must then make decisions to change. It is worth mentioning that change is not easy; it requires knowledge and a strong will to support a cause. But it is worth it.

When Josef Albers fled Europe before World War II, he inspired a new kind of art in the United States. So too must architects today borrow ideas from one another to develop them and create new art. Times are changing and young architects now have great skills with sophisticated digital technologies. But they must mix these new technologies with old ways to add real value to society.

Yung Ho Chang
Founder, Atelier Feichang Jianzhu (FCJZ), Beijing

→ Have faith in your work

By 1991, I had been drawing or making paper architecture for roughly eight years. At that point, I was working on a series of site-less houses for imaginary clients, typically an artist or a writer. However hypothetical they were, I treated them as if they were real commissions, making drawings and models, developing and revising the designs time and time again. These exercises were very important, because they allowed me to explore and understand the relationship between space, structure, and scenario (meaning life scenes). I don't like words such as "use," "function," or "program," which all seem too cold. Focusing on a dwelling with four rooms (living, dining/kitchen, bed, and bath), I designed lifestyle at the same time as structure and space. Time went on and I had no idea whether these houses would ever be built.

In 2013, my partner, Lijia Lu, and I revisited the Vertical Glass House, a project I had designed in 1991 as an entry to a competition run by the

Japanese magazine *Shinkenchiku*. We submitted it to the West Bund Biennial of Architecture and Contemporary Art, a large-scale exhibition in Shanghai that was planning to build a series of freestanding pavilions along the Huangpu River. The Biennial accepted it and built it according to the original scheme. It is now used essentially as a studio-guesthouse and will open to the public as a café in the near future.

Then in 2022, three of the houses I had conceived thirty years earlier were built as part of a complex in Ningbo called the Education Forum and are now used as guesthouses and spaces for exhibitions and classes.

We feel very lucky about these old schemes coming to life. But luck alone wasn't enough. We had faith in our architecture.

VALUES

Carol Ross Barney
Founding design principal, Ross Barney Architects, Chicago

→ Design matters

Design always matters. Not just when it's affordable or convenient. It matters all the time.

Design excellence—living in an environment that is truly uplifting—isn't a privilege that only some people get to enjoy. Good design is a right in our democratic society.

Size and prestige don't matter. A lot of the projects we work on can probably be classified as noble projects, meaning that they don't have big budgets and they certainly were not the most publicized or anticipated projects. But they are important in their communities.

We do our best work for projects where design may not be expected: projects that you find at the very edges or sometimes in the margins, but ones that affect the quality of daily life and need innovative solutions.

Design is problem solving. If a solution is simple, constructible, and integrated, then it is beautiful. Originality is overrated, but innovation is essential to elegant and progressive design.

Design is a team sport. Don't work alone and don't take yourself too seriously. The best design leaders are able to see value in multiple ideas and approaches. They promote and weave those concepts into a better whole.

Architecture isn't ever easy. If I am completely honest, architecture has never loved me as much I love architecture. What doesn't kill you makes you stronger, and the joy and fulfillment of making space has wiped out any disappointment or regret.

Every day, every drawing, every project is a new challenge.

Li Hu
Founding partner, Open Architecture, Beijing

→ Develop yourself

Over the years, I have realized more and more clearly that it is more important for an architect (or just about anybody in a field of artistic creation) to develop as a person, not just as a professional.

Ultimately, if you work honestly, then the work itself is the reflection of who you are, your understanding of the world around you, your true understanding and affection for nature, and how you see the way society works. Though seemingly large and vague, these issues drive every decision an architect makes in any design process. They range from how and where to choose to build, how many resources it takes to construct and operate a building, what impact that building brings to society and the environment, and what story it tells the public. A building's attitude is a reflection of the architect's mindset—modest or flamboyant, deep or trendy, exclusive or generous.

How you develop yourself over a lifetime is a process of getting to know yourself—to discover what you truly believe in, what you truly long for. You will be influenced by your encounters, your mentors, your friends, the books you read, the events you experience, the places where you travel. These encounters are partly accidental, but not entirely. You are attracted to what you hope to become and what you want to be part of. This process of development by chance and by choice makes you who you are. And that, in turn, influences what you do in architecture.

Christos Passas
Director, Zaha Hadid Architects, London

→ Take care of the earth

Humanity has existed on this beautiful planet for many centuries and has created amazing architectural marvels that tell us something bigger about ourselves—helping us understand our history, our deep human values, and how we respond to the challenges of each era, ultimately marking our journey in time.

In the twenty-first century, humanity has become, whether we like it or not, the steward of the planet. We are now largely responsible for a number of challenging areas that directly impact our ability to sustain life and well-being on our home planet.

Our generation and future generations must think individually and collectively, at an eco-technological level, on how to meet these challenges.

Remember to embrace the difficulties, and engage with hope and positive vision.

As architects, we must burn with passion and flow with energy to try the untested and continue to experiment fearlessly despite all the failures.

Bring your own unique talents into this world and work hard to express the richness of human diversity.

Believe that in the end your journey will reward you for the things you know, and more importantly, the things you don't yet know.

Are you ready?

Liu Thai Ker
Chairman, Morrow Architects and Planners, Singapore

→ Serve humanity

I. M. Pei once told me: "There is no function without beauty." I also believe there is no beauty without function.

As architecture is built of steel and concrete, we must design our buildings with durable beauty so they remain valued for generations.

Just as no man is an island, no building is an island. Design your projects to harmonize with surrounding buildings, just as singers do in a choral group, with a few soloists standing out.

Architectural design is communication without words. It must express function by its combination of geometric forms and good proportions.

Design your buildings with modernity, locality, and ethnicity in mind. Use modern materials and technology, while considering local climate, customs, and conditions, while capturing indigenous design genes. Remember: today's historical buildings are modern buildings of the past. Good modern buildings are the heritage of the future.

Instead of pursuing fame, try to serve the well-being of users, the environment, and the city. If you do your job well, then you may become famous someday.

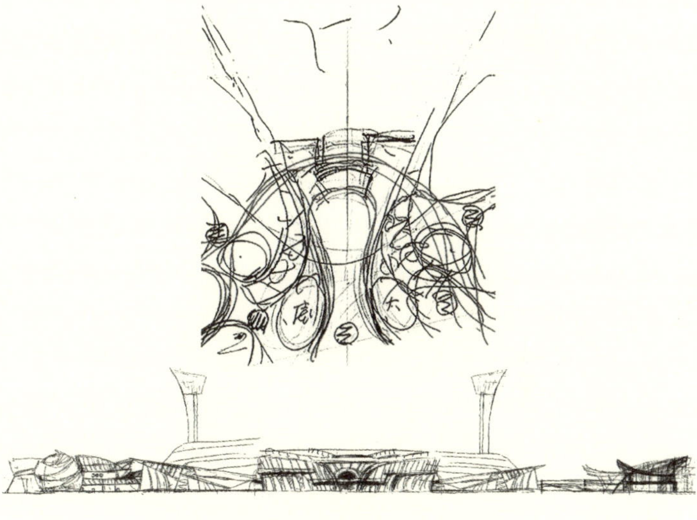

Weifang Art Centre, Shandong Province, China

Rocco Yim

Founding principal, Rocco Yim Design Architects, Hong Kong

→ Make a choice

Who am I to give budding architects and practitioners a sermon on aspirations?

That is not my intention. I simply wish to pose a direct question to provoke thinking: Do you want to be successful or do you want to be good?

To be successful—meaning you are rewarded with riches and fame—you need to prioritize capturing the trends, courting the media, creating the "wow."

To be good—meaning you care about enriching the lives of others and contributing to the collective well-being of our environment—you need to be empathetic to the needs of humble folks and sensitive to the effective use of our resources, willing to turn out "thoughtful" architecture, even if it is modest and self-effacing. Obviously, this may not bring immediate fame or wealth, but it may ensure sustained value in your work and maybe, just maybe, one day it gets "discovered" and appreciated.

You may say that you can be both successful and good. Sure. In that case, you are blessed with a rare gift on par with some (not all, mind you) of the masters. In which case, why waste your time reading my stuff?

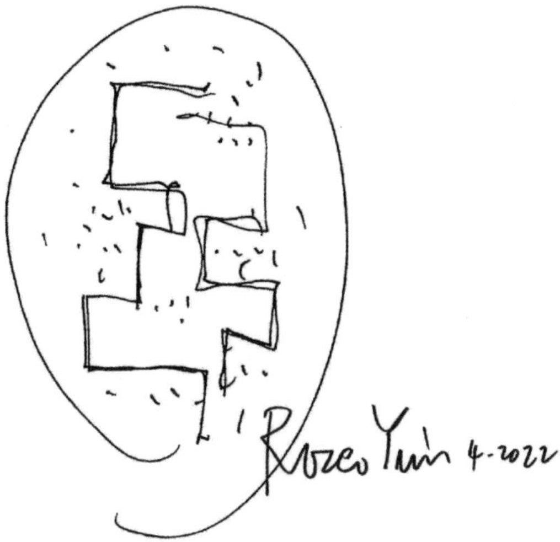

Huawei Conference Villas, Shenzhen, China

Wang Hui
Founding principal, Urbanus, Beijing

→ Learn how to say "no"

It would be terrible for an architect never to learn how to say "no." If everything is "yes," then you can hardly be yourself. The most important time to say "no" is when you are successful, when you are offered too many opportunities. If you accept them all, then you jeopardize the ones already in hand.

Another critical time to say "no" is when you do not have enough projects, when every opportunity is a temptation or even a rescue. However, if you say "yes" without analyzing the long-term value, then you will lose one of the best opportunities to remain steady and reflect. Years later, you may look back on past successes and failures and sigh at how nice it would have been if you had said "no" in a timely fashion. Saying "no" is definitely an art and a technique that takes a long time to acquire. It is best to learn it at a young age.

Cui Kai
Honorary president and chief architect, China Architecture Design & Research Group (CADG), Beijing, and founder and chief architect, Land-Based Rationalism Design & Research Center of CADG, Beijing

→ Respect nature

Your design attitude should encompass respect and goodwill for nature, context, and life.

Your design responsibility should involve concern for and commitment to problem-solving, technology, and quality.

Stephen Cassell, Kim Yao,
and Adam Yarinsky
Principals, Architecture Research Office
(ARO), New York

→ Keep learning

Learning is the core of our practice. We continually seek to grow—whether by taking on diverse project types, listening to the communities we build in, collaborating in the office, or teaching the next generation of architects. Our design process is rooted in inquiry and stems from our belief that deep understanding creates transformational architecture. Learning also keeps us engaged in our work, each other, and the world.

Within each project, we work iteratively to develop and assess alternatives, gaining shared insights directly from drawings, models, and mock-ups. Our process is holistic—from analyzing site information, to diagramming program relationships, to developing formal strategies, to exploring material qualities. Communicating clearly to ourselves and to people involved with or affected by our work is an essential aspect of learning. Learning from ourselves, collaborators, and communities enriches how we work together, makes for better architecture, and enables our practice to constantly evolve.

V-Soleil facade shading prototype

Steve McConnell
Board chair and managing partner,
NBBJ, Seattle

→ Seek perspective

On January 13, 2022, I stood on a remote saddle high in the Ellsworth Mountains, Antarctica. It was -20°F. The view was infinite and amazing. Spectacular peaks captivated my imagination, and glaciers averaging six thousand feet deep spanned the horizon. I stood at the very edge of the earth—an extreme place to be, yet one so remote that I could not deny the perspective it offered on life and our planet.

To be there, a place of rock, ice, silence, and extreme cold, was to know self-reliance, awe, and how fragile life can be. Still, something inexplicable was happening—it had snowed several inches the night before and soon I would discover a raging storm was brewing.

Antarctica is a desert—the driest continent, with an average precipitation of one and a half inches per year. Yet more than a foot of snow fell over the two weeks I was in the Ellsworth Mountains. "Yes, our climate is changing,"

I thought. "This snowstorm should not be happening." A few days later at high camp another storm raged on and I wondered whether intense 60-mph winds would accelerate and endanger my life, and whether climate change was the culprit. That day, in that moment, I feared climate change.

My adventure became a personal field study, clarifying what I had sensed, read, and heard about climate change—and a powerful affirmation of the value of perspective earned to bond knowing and purpose.

Seek perspective.

Be a purpose-driven architect.

Lawrence Scarpa

Principal, Brooks + Scarpa, Los Angeles

→ Follow a vision that echoes your values

Passion trumps privilege: success doesn't come from pedigree. I'm proof of that. My father, an Italian immigrant, worked hard to build a life while raising four kids by himself. Your passion for architecture will carry you farther than any inherited privilege. Commit to your craft relentlessly.

Innovate or stagnate: the world evolves, and so must you. Embrace innovation; it's the lifeblood of architecture. Sustainable practices, technology integration, and cutting-edge concepts will set your work apart.

Balance tradition and progress: respect the past, but don't be bound by it. Architecture thrives on tradition and innovation dancing together. Blend timeless principles with contemporary culture, creating designs that resonate across generations.

Leadership is service: involve yourself with others who are trying to change the world. You can serve society with a vision that is collectively pursued. True leadership inspires, motivates, and amplifies everyone's strengths.

Listen but don't follow: everyone will have an opinion. Listen and learn but don't follow. It is okay to be different and pursue your own vision and try new things. In life you will regret more the things that you haven't done than the mistakes you've made. Mistakes are just iterations, not failures.

Awards follow excellence: focus on excellence, not accolades. Awards are by-products of dedication and quality work.

Be local but think globally: my journey began in a small central Florida town of fewer than twenty thousand people, but I believed I could have a bigger impact on our world. Don't be afraid to think globally; design transcends boundaries. Your ideas can shape environments far beyond your immediate surroundings.

Man and Nature by Calvin Tsao

Calvin Tsao

Founding principal, Tsao & McKown Architects, Brooklyn, New York

→ Be alert to the world and its needs

As you enter the professional sphere, it is important to acknowledge that as an architect you not only answer to your career and ambitions but also bear the responsibility to defend, if not foster, civic good. This is more urgent today than ever, as human existence has been challenged by social and environmental vulnerabilities.

It is important to take this responsibility earnestly. Architecture is the principal actor on and protector of the built environment. Its health, resilience, and sustainability are in your hands.

As architects, we should draw on not only our craft but also its theoretical constructs. We must be alert to the world we live in—its needs, aspirations, and challenges.

We are gatekeepers to our physical world, not just for our own agenda but for the whole of our society.

That is the key to making lasting architecture.

ENGAGEMENT

Gordon Gill
Partner, Adrian Smith + Gordon Gill Architecture, Chicago

→ Think, believe, act

Think:

Approach your work with an inclusive and global perspective. Think about people, the global environment, and the issues that, as individuals and as communities, we all face around the world.

Listen to the larger needs of your global society and don't impose preconceived ideas.

Translate your knowledge through your work and find opportunities that broaden your perspective on solving problems. Think about people. Think about nature. Think about technology. Think about time. Be a bridge to the future.

Define the problem at hand and offer creative and realistic solutions.

Believe:

Approach your work with conviction and sincerity. Belief doesn't mean inflexibility. Be honest about your work and be critically constructive of yourself and others. Understand how your work has value to others.

Leave behind more than you found.

Test ideas constantly and always keep learning.

Consider the impact of your work on the centuries to come.

Try to create architecture that stands the test of time.

The work will evolve.

Never worry about populism.

Act:

Find things that get you excited. Work with people whom you trust, who are creative and honest. Think well into the future, beyond your own knowledge, and discover what might be. This is a long game. Experiment, research, and dream. Make your dreams happen. Don't leave them as abstract ideas. Don't procrastinate.

When you act, share. Sharing knowledge and helping others strengthens the dialogue of practice and communities.

This is your job; this is your life.

Enjoy every minute of it.

Michel Rojkind
Founder, Rojkind Arquitectos,
Mexico City

→ Weave the fabric of communities

As you begin your journey in architecture, understand that you're embarking on a path of profound influence—not just on landscapes but on lives, communities, and our living planet. In my practice, I've learned that architecture is about fostering connections, nurturing spaces that bring people together, and creating environments that give back more than they take.

Your creativity in this field should transcend traditional design thinking. It's about weaving the fabric of communities, understanding and amplifying the voices of those who will live within the spaces you create. It's about connecting art, science, and technology, and embracing the most advanced tools to help you bridge digital design with local fabrication.

Remember, the responsibility of an architect is to serve and uplift communities. Every project you undertake is a chance to regenerate and rejuvenate not just a physical space but the human spirit.

Strive to create places where communities can thrive, where connection and interaction are facilitated, and where every individual feels a sense of belonging and empowerment.

The future of architecture is about crafting legacies of positive impact, spaces that resonate with care, compassion, and an unwavering commitment to enhancing communal well-being and a profound reciprocal relationship to our planet.

Architects have a strong responsibility as shape-shifters of the future. You can manifest in the material world something that you once only imagined. What you build will, in turn, build you—strengthening your character and understanding as architects and humans. Your journey is about more than construction; it's a process of crafting hope, nurturing relationships, and envisioning a world enriched by your contributions.

Ministry of Culture Bujairi Development, Riyadh, Saudi Arabia

Rasem Badran
Founder, Badran Design Studio,
Amman, Jordan

→ Make connections

Architecture is a micro-city of connections and relationships among people as well as with the larger world. It's about spaces and how people live there with respect to time, seasons, traditions, development, and context. Young architects don't need rules to follow but should instead learn from feeling what is around them in those micro-cities and spaces.

Carlo Ratti
Founding partner, Carlo Ratti Associati, Turin, and director, MIT Senseable City Lab, Cambridge, Massachusetts

→ Redefine architecture to address the great challenges we face

"The first right on earth is the right of the ego," writes Ayn Rand in *The Fountainhead* (1943), which celebrates the idea of the twentieth-century architect. During the course of my career, I have come to learn that this idea—which is driven by what we could call a "Promethean" vision of architecture—no longer applies. We need to learn how to work in new, collaborative ways.

Architecture has to change with the times. In *Toward an Architecture* (1923), Le Corbusier posed the question of redefining architecture so that it could become an expression of the industrial society. More than a hundred years later, architecture needs to redefine itself again. Such change is triggered not only by the pandemic that ravaged our way of living in recent years but also by the great challenges we face—from climate change to urban segregation.

The discipline we all learned at school as "architecture" no longer suffices by itself to respond to these challenges. Young architects should see themselves as "choral architects," a term I started using in my book with Matthew Claudel, *Open Source Architecture* (2014). We need to venture farther out and absorb knowledge from other disciplines. For those who are just starting and growing their own firms, such a transdisciplinary approach will help them mobilize experts and communities from different fields to solve problems on the urban, national, and global scales.

Marble Curtain

Jeanne Gang
Founding principal and partner,
Studio Gang, Chicago

→ Be curious and authentic

Architecture is about being deeply curious. When you're endlessly fascinated with the project at hand, many questions will arise. Identifying the uncertainties and struggling with them is, I think, far more satisfying than honing a groove or becoming excessively confident. Design is essentially about finding a way to put your questions into a given project. You may even self-initiate projects because of your own burning questions. Your best questions will be relevant to others, as well.

It also helps to be curious about yourself. Interrogate your own motivations for wanting to be in architecture: What drives you? After all your years of architectural education, what is the thing you have that no one else can teach you? Your authenticity comes from cultivating that unique thing.

PROCESS

Odile Decq

Founder, Studio Odile Decq and
Confluence Institute, Paris

→ **Appreciate now.**

→ **Enjoy the present time.
It may not last.**

→ **Stay safe.**

→ **Keep dreaming.**

Elizabeth Diller
Partner, Diller Scofidio + Renfro,
New York

→ Put yourself out there

Never settle on simply being a problem solver. Be a maker of problems worth solving. And don't ever let the words "risk management" enter your vocabulary. Persevere to build your work and put yourself out there. Don't wait for the opportunity—steal or borrow a site if you have to.

Don't just throw bombs from afar—something I was certainly guilty of early on. Rather than staying at the periphery, place yourself in the center of it all where you can actually get things done. To realize the High Line, my studio worked with the New York City government and the Bloomberg administration. It helps when there's an alignment of open-minded administration with your goals. If you can, take a seat at the table with the grown-ups.

Hina Jamelle and Ali Rahim
Directors, Contemporary Architecture Practice, New York and Shanghai

→ Embrace your expertise

Use your knowledge of the discipline to focus on a goal and work hard from every angle to achieve it. Allow your aims to evolve and change as you grow as an architect. Stay true to who you are as an individual and develop your strengths from your own unique perspective and aspirations, which are your greatest assets. When you embrace your expertise and the power of your voice, you can cultivate innovative design research and methodologies. This will give you a unique signature that sets you apart from others in the field. Remember that new architecture is designed in the present but exists in the future. Orient your work toward the future of society.

As you build your practice, it is crucial to develop strong business skills. Do not let the perceived trade-off between good business and good design influence your decisions. Instead, strive to excel in both areas. Business will follow if you stay true to your design goals and demand your worth. To expand and test the limits of your work, it is essential to cross cultural boundaries and contexts. This requires a deep openness, appreciation, and understanding of the nuances of different cultures and ways of life. Remember to remain nimble and flexible, as each situation presents different challenges. Stay humble and focused, and always strive to achieve the best work you can.

James Wines
Founder, SITE, New York

→ Never stop questioning

Apply the harshest levels of criticism to everything you do. For any designer intent on breaking new ground this is essential, as well as the most difficult. It basically entails questioning every derivative idea, conventional standard, stylistic persuasion, and traditional paradigm for polite design. This means rejecting all those comfortable temptations to embrace some form of "if-you-please" good taste. Marcel Duchamp allegedly said, "I have forced myself to contradict myself, in order to avoid conforming to my own taste."

One of the fundamental qualifications for designing future buildings and public spaces is applying an "economy of means." Picasso reportedly advised, "Forcing yourself to use restricted means is the sort of restraint that liberates invention. It obliges you to make a kind of progress you can't even imagine in advance." In architecture and urban design, this reductive sensibility opens up fertile levels of frugality that can eliminate waste and expand visual imagination. It can encourage new aesthetic experiences that are the polar opposite of today's proclivity for bombastic sculptural solutions and, instead, liberate designers' exploration of new sources of content.

Go back to basics and never stop questioning routinely sanctioned career formulas. There are pervasive and seductive temptations in the realm of "good design" that only encourage an endless pattern of creative forfeiture, economic imprudence, and resource depletion. My advice is most applicable to those who have the courage to pursue their visions in a climate of risk.

Drawing by Richard Hassell

Richard Hassell and Mun Summ Wong
Founding directors, WOHA, Singapore

→ Get lost

When you are a young designer, there are so many interesting ideas to follow, it is easy to wind up spending endless time on unproductive dead ends.

The good news is that you will learn to recognize these resource-sapping diversions through experience and to see in advance which pathways are new and which have potential. This means as you get older you can spend your time much more productively.

The bad news is that this early-warning system can only be acquired through thousands of hours of being lost in the maze.

A compensation for all these hours is the realization that some of these wandering wonderings will stick with you as a pathway with great potential, even though at the time the way may have been blocked. You can come back to them years later and find your way through the maze with your hard-earned sense of direction.

Marion Weiss and Michael Manfredi
Founders, Weiss/Manfredi, New York

→ View each project as an opportunity for intellectual adventure

As architects, we believe the necessity for production is an excuse for research and exploration. Every project is an opportunity to learn about embedded histories, new conditions, people, and programs, and simultaneously transcend what has been done before and invent new designs that have yet to be imagined.

Think synthetically and act creatively. Thinking broadly—beyond disciplinary blinders—while acting precisely is becoming especially urgent as our environment's resources are increasingly limited. We continually remind ourselves that no task is too small or inconsequential, nor too large, to merit critical questions and creative exploration. Each time we engage with contemporary challenges, no matter the scale, we allow ourselves the opportunity for growth and innovation.

Remember that our position as designers requires us to consistently rise to the enduring fact that our world is made immeasurably richer by design. To understand the evolving challenges that impact the fragile balance of the world we engage in today means asking big questions and taking actions as designers to shape a more ethical, equitable, and resilient built environment.

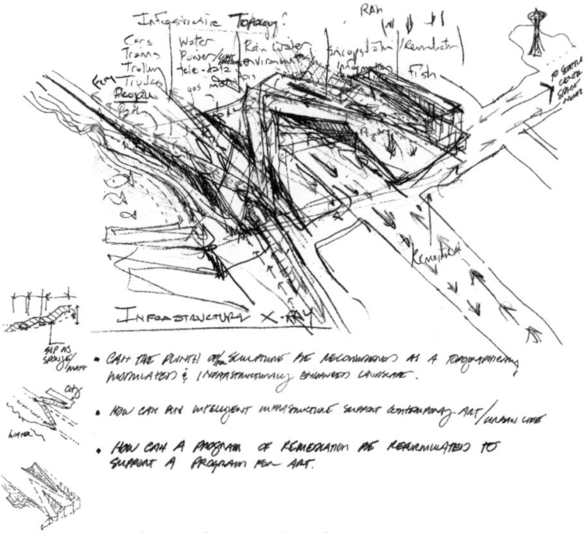

Olympic Sculpture Park, Seattle, Washington

Experimental House R128, Stuttgart, Germany

Werner Sobek
Founder, Werner Sobek AG,
Stuttgart, Germany

→ Build your dream, even if it's "impossible"

Believe only what you have verified for yourself. This is the most important advice of all.

Many people told me that my private residence, R128, was an impossible dream. Fully transparent, completely recyclable, relying only on energy from renewable sources, and much lighter than traditional buildings, it started as a vision. I began with a steep plot at the edge of Stuttgart, a property that was deemed unbuildable by many of my colleagues. I have been living in this house for twenty-five years now—and I still enjoy every single day in this gem of contemporary architecture.

William Pedersen
Co-founder, Kohn Pedersen Fox (KPF), New York

→ Design comparatively

As a young architect, I was placed in charge of the design for a major academic institution. It was my first opportunity to work with a client as the leader of a design team. Having spent the previous three years working with I. M. Pei on the National Gallery in Washington, D.C., I assumed his method of introducing a concept to a client would be mine. But . . . I was certainly not of Pei's stature nor had I been selected as the architect by the client. I was representing the architect selected.

Confidently I strode into my first encounter with the client, armed with what I thought was "the solution." I presented it well. However, it was not received well. In fact, it was brutally rejected. So negative was the response that our future role was put in question.

I needed to rethink my method. It was then that I decided to design comparatively. I would present a series of responses to the program.

I wasn't intending to offer a menu from which the client could pick and choose, but to use the conversation that emerged from comparing the various schemes to better understand the client and for them to better understand my intentions. It worked brilliantly. I learned about their aspirations. They learned about mine. A better design evolved. It was not one of those originally presented but was brought about by our mutual blending of goals. Within our architectural team, dialogue also was stimulated. Each team member was encouraged to contribute—not just to follow.

During the past fifty years the comparative process has been my method. Documentation of its success is recorded in my book *Gesture and Response* (2021).

Xu Tiantian
Founder, DnA_Design and Architecture, Beijing

→ Look beyond the city

Although I live in Beijing, I have spent much of the past decade working on projects in the countryside in places like Songyang County in Zhejiang Province. Rural revitalization is a critical need in China and countries around the world. It requires not just constructing buildings in rural regions but integrating the economic, social, and cultural aspects of these places to create a more synthetic complexity.

To do this in Songyang, we have employed what we call "architectural acupuncture," an approach that applies design pressure at key locations to strengthen the community as a whole. It introduces public programs—sometimes quite small—to rural areas as a way of restoring village identity, recapturing historical and cultural context, and stimulating economic growth. It's a holistic approach.

Rural public architecture is a new typology with few specific codes or parameters for reference. We need to invent much of what we do and learn by trial and error. Any flaws in the design process need to be followed up in later stages.

We have learned to listen and then think creatively. When the head of a particular village in Sonyang invited us to create a bamboo pavilion, we studied the material and investigated its properties. We discovered that the bamboo most often used for construction can only be harvested in the fall and winter and requires a time-consuming and labor- intensive process. But Moso bamboo has sturdy roots that spread horizontally and offers the opportunity to use plants grown on site to form a structure. No material needed to be purchased or transported. No construction was required. We simply wove live bamboo into a gracefully bending enclosure for an outdoor theater space.

All these rural projects emerge from daily observations. On one hand, we need rational thinking and logic; on the other, we need to trust our intuition and instinct. Some judgments are made prior to reason and linguistics.

The more restrictions there are, the more you need to look for clues. This is both a challenge and an opportunity, and you must overcome ordinary, stagnant thinking.

Ken Yeang
Executive director, T. R. Hamzah & Yeang, Kuala Lumpur and London

→ Focus

I believe a key factor for success is focus. I have asked many who have achieved immense success for tips, and the most common are: stay close to the knitting and stay the path. It's about focusing on one's mission and doing it extremely well.

Multitasking is a vicissitude of being an architect. Architects must undertake a wide scope, from design to delivery. They must perform a multitude of functions: getting the business (marketing), doing the business (professional services), running the business (business management), and funding the business (financial management). Doing each well and all at once makes an architect's life very stressful.

An architect cannot be everything to everybody but can be 100 percent to a select few and less to others. Architects can approach the business by focusing on one of these types of firms: design-focused, service-focused, or production-focused. Emphasis on one does not mean ineffectiveness in others. It just means being best known for one aspect, whether for design or service or production.

For instance, as a design-focused practice, my firm is driven by green design to save the planet from environmental catastrophe. We have not deviated from this for five decades. Focus enables continuous improvements, knowledge advancements, design skills honing, and staying on the cutting edge.

Solaris, Singapore

Mark Jensen
Founding principal, Jensen Architects,
San Francisco

→ Ideas > Image

Ideas should precede image. In an image-obsessed, short-attention-span culture that commonly wades into the shallows, this is a radical idea for architecture. It is easy to reach straight for the reference images (pictures) grabbed from the internet. More difficult but more rewarding is the search for ideas through curiosity and contemplation.

So, what is the nature of the architectural idea in this context? It can be found in the full and deep inquiry into the situation of the project. And the situation? It is more than site, program, code, and style. It is also the interaction of the eventual built work with people's lives, with the broader social and cultural context, and with the health of our natural environment. The search for the simplest and clearest ideas that stitch together and converse with these aspects of the situation is where intention resides. Only then will the image of the work reveal itself.

Yes, architects are service providers who must skillfully apply the technologies of our trade. But, if we choose to do so, then we can also engage in cultural production. If we only provide service and sampled image, then there are emerging technologies that will render our profession obsolete. We should instead cultivate curiosity about deeper purposes, responsibilities, and cultural meanings in building. And we should even aspire for beauty, not only in consumable images but also in the ineffable qualities of well-composed space and material atmosphere revealed over time.

Qingyun Ma
Founder, MADA s.p.a.m., Los Angeles and Xi'an, China

→ Push toward the edge and beyond

Architecture requires patience and conscience, which lie on a foundation of creativity and innovation. When creativity is doubted and innovation overlooked, one's mind and hand are dulled and can't push toward the edge or beyond to a new horizon. As an architect, you must resist a society that betrays us by defaulting to normality. Align your curiosities with the common goal of others.

Kaoru Mende
CEO, Lighting Planners Associates,
Tokyo

→ Capture the ephemeral

Light and shadow are important design tools. Use them.

Light is material and is as important as metal, stone, wood, concrete, or glass. It can improve the quality of any space.

People and architecture should be lit. Time is visualized by light. The function of space defines the character of light. Light creates an atmosphere beyond function. Designing shadow = light. Always design light ecologically.

Hitoshi Abe
Founder, Atelier Hitoshi Abe,
Sendai, Japan, and Los Angeles

→ Keep opposites in balance

There are always two roles to play in the profession of architecture. The first is to strengthen and sustain the discipline by pursuing the best possible building design, as defined by the professional community. It is a traditional way for architects to practice.

The second role, however, contradicts the first. It demands that you question the established practices of the discipline and explore the possibility of expanding and redefining them in the future. This is a difficult task, as it requires you to address an unknown future in opposition to established practices. It asks you to be the producer of knowledge rather than the consumer. As aggressive technological developments and a changing global economy have brought a paradigm shift in our world and increased the need to redefine our discipline, the latter role has gained greater importance.

As an architect, you must constantly balance these opposite roles—being both upholder of the discipline and revolutionary, dealing with both the past and the future.

Miyagi Water Tower, Rifu, Miyagi Prefecture, Japan

Ignacio Gomez
Global design principal, Aedas, Dubai

→ Be methodical

Take a moment to critically examine your preconceived ideas and inherent biases. Steer clear of moving too quickly toward design responses. Early ideas often stem from personal experiences, which can subtly limit your capacity to envision diverse and innovative architectural solutions.

Consider architecture as a practice grounded in research and methodical processes. It's about more than just constructing buildings; it's about pioneering new design trajectories. Enter each project with a mindset open to inquiry, allowing the design to unfold through a process of deliberate experimentation, rather than focusing on a predetermined conclusion from the beginning.

Broaden your skill set with a variety of tools and techniques, such as drawing, 3D modeling, rendering, and editing. A comprehensive tool kit enables you to navigate the various challenges and directions in which your architectural endeavors may unfold. Encountering periods of uncertainty or discomfort is part of this developmental process. These moments are catalysts for growth and innovation. Stay dedicated to your methodology and consistently refine your tools, opening the door to unanticipated design possibilities and allowing a project to dictate its own purpose and raison d'être. Don't impose; just follow it.

Venture into new realms and contemplate ideas that might initially appear unconventional or unorthodox. Persistence is crucial; if a strategy doesn't work initially, then revisit it with new insights and determination.

Finally, don't limit yourself to a single style or method. Develop a versatile and evolving process, supported by a wide array of tools and techniques. This will not only expand your architectural skills but also enrich the developmental process of your projects.

Don't have a style; have a process and let it be.

Sketch by Arthur Andersson of the Basilica di Sant'Andrea in Mantua, Italy

F. Christian Wise
Founding principal, Andersson/Wise,
Austin, Texas

→ Don't be precious with your ideas

Iterate, iterate, and iterate again. Don't be precious with your ideas and especially with your drawings and representations. Such tools are a means to an end—doing good buildings—unless you just want to do drawings and representations. Keep revising, and every once in a while you might go beyond good.

Zhu Pei
Founder, Studio Zhu Pei, Beijing, and dean, Central Academy of Fine Arts, School of Architecture, Beijing

→ View artificial intelligence as an asset, not an enemy

Will architecture and architects be replaced by artificial intelligence and digital technology? This is a hot topic among students and architects. My answer is no. Architecture is art and the most important creative activity of humanity. Unlike painting, poetry, music, sculpture, and other arts, architecture, as the oldest art of humanity, is rooted in the natural environment of mountains, rivers, sunlight, wind, gravity, and other elements that we rely on for survival. It is a construction art related to human beings, nature, space, and materials. As long as we need to live in the real world and factors such as gravity and sunlight have not changed, and we have not mutated as living organisms, then the nature of architecture will not change, and the creative work of architects will not be replaced by artificial intelligence or digital technology. On the contrary, the challenges of artificial intelligence and digital technology will inspire and help architects to think more deeply about creativity and intelligent construction.

Jingdezhen Imperial Kiln Museum, Jingdezhen, China

Arthur Gensler

Founder, Gensler, San Francisco

From *Art's Principles: 50 Years of Hard-Learned Lessons in Building a World-Class Professional Services Firm* (2015)

→ Give responsibility plus authority

Very smart people want to make use of their talents. They are hungry for responsibility and welcome the chance to flex their minds. Challenging assignments give them an opportunity to grow.

You should do everything possible to empower talent [in your firm] to serve your clients and represent your firm in the most positive way possible. The key to unlocking your talents' potential is to make sure they are given the authority they need to succeed. Authority enables them to access resources and make decisions that help advance the firm.

Some managers are afraid to empower others. If you are one of these leaders, I suggest you offer levels of authority. As your talent makes wise decisions, you can grant greater levels of authority.

Always match the responsibilities you give them with the right amount of authority to get the job done.

Also, I have observed that most service professionals suffer from a major blind spot: they invest heavily to become great technicians, but they have little knowledge about business. The earlier you learn business skills, the better.

PERSONAL DEVELOPMENT

Sahar Kharrufa
Professor of architecture, Ajman University, United Arab Emirates

→ Take risks

Gain experience any way you can.

Widen the scope of your experience. Don't define yourself by one field of expertise.

Don't be afraid to take risks. With great risks come great rewards.

There is nothing wrong about changing direction. Very few people stick with the same goals all their life.

Always improve yourself.

Engage others in your work.

Publicize yourself.

Launch your own website.

Samer Charara
Principal, Woods Bagot, Dubai

→ Make your own story

Passion is an attitude; skill is learned. Make your own story.

Tobias Wallisser
Co-founder, LAVA, Berlin, and professor, State Academy of Fine Arts, Stuttgart

→ Be authentic

Believe in yourself and be true to your beliefs. Architecture must be authentic and done with future users in mind because it's a great responsibility to shape an environment.

Nader Tehrani
Founding principal, NADAAA, Boston

→ Be curious

Listen carefully—but don't forget to translate what you hear into formal, spatial, and material terms.

Techniques are not ideas, but there are moments when the instrumentality of techniques produce the very ideas at stake.

Work on overtime—for yourself, that is.

Design—not just at your desk but while you run.

Learn how the trades work—then redesign your means and methods accordingly.

Don't just eat—prepare the meal for others.

People matter—and the discipline of architecture does too. Don't let them tell you they are mutually exclusive.

You don't need advice from me, but history does offer a treasure trove of lessons to be interpreted and translated. If you're not already, learn how to become curious.

Tips don't come from the top, they come from the trenches.

Marlon Blackwell
Principal, Marlon Blackwell Architects, Fayetteville, Arkansas

→ Draw from drawing

All kinds of newer, shinier ways to make buildings will evolve in your life, but none are as important or as influential as simply drawing. Drawing is essential and indispensable, gathering the forces and influences of your life. It is the Seine through which ideas are floated and filtered, the refinery for distillation and purification. Draw until it becomes involuntary, a habit, a need, a compulsion. Drawing will give you more than you can imagine.

Travel at every opportunity. See the canon, but also go to obscure places in pursuit of authentic cultures and shared humanity. There is a generosity of spirit that comes from travel, an appreciation of what each place has to offer, and a font source of ideas for making your own place better.

Ambition alone will not be enough, nor will a strong work ethic, though these are essential. Eventually, a bit of pretense is needed too, the kind that gives you the courage to write to your heroes, to share your work with publishers, to teach with legends. And while talent is certainly important, it's not nearly so important as willpower and the dedication to a slow, patient search for true things, the sublime.

Opportunities won't always be obvious, whether architectural or geographical. By believing that architecture can happen anywhere, at any scale and for anyone, a world of possibilities opens. Many good and even some great ideas won't materialize, but fortunately they go back into your "spiritual savings bank," a font of possibilities and inspiration to draw from, to embed in later work. An opportunity lost is not an idea lost.

Ralf Steinhauer
Director, RSP Architects Planners & Engineers, Dubai

→ Find a mentor

Embrace your passion for architecture. Let your passion for design be the heartbeat and the guidance of your career. Remember, in architecture, true fulfillment arises from the spaces you create and not necessarily from the pursuit of fame or fortune.

First, seek out a mentor who possesses a wealth of industry knowledge, someone who can impart invaluable insights beyond the scope of your academic training.

Second, never hesitate to ask questions. Embrace new learning opportunities to avoid feeling like you are in a *Groundhog Day* situation. Architecture is a journey of continuous growth and discovery, where every day is a chance to evolve and expand your horizons.

Third, establish your own key performance indicators. Let these serve as both a motivational tool and a means of self-reflection, keeping you aligned with your professional goals.

And finally, always remember that being an architect is a unique and fulfilling journey. Even on challenging days, recognize the noble privilege of being able to design and shape the world around us.

Drawing by Richard Fenne

Richard Fenne
Director, Woods Bagot, Dubai

→ Keep changing

Every challenge you'll face in the architectural profession—whether good or bad—is an opportunity to learn. The beauty of our profession is that it constantly evolves. So being open-minded to change keeps you relevant and broadens your knowledge base. Clients might be paying by the hour, but what you're selling is the value of many years of learning and knowledge gathering.

John Ruble

Partner, Moore Ruble Yudell Architects and Planners, Santa Monica, California

→ Strive to be multimodal

We all know that architecture school can be a cruel rite of passage. Often enough it seems only to reward the exceptionally visual and conceptually talented, even discouraging others from carrying on. If nothing else, it toughens you up. A student teaching assistant of mine at Cornell put it this way: *Start trusting your own sensibilities or get lost, baby!*

But now that you've gotten this far, here's one thing to consider going forward. The world likes to think of us as a *type* (check out the 1998 movie *There's Something About Mary* for a good example). But the fact is, we architects are a very broad-spectrum bunch. We come from all kinds of backgrounds, and therefore we bring different perspectives to the many divine challenges of the profession. Whatever your own origin story is, know that you are valuable and needed. You may have a head for management, be a dreamer and a visionary, a tech wizard, an intuitive sculptor, or a gifted communicator. Architecture needs all of that and more, and the world needs it from us. Whatever you learned in school, you will soon see how urgent all these abilities are. And it's important that you recognize and nurture them, in yourself and in others. Strive to be multimodal, to acquire the skills that don't come easily. That, and learn to work brilliantly with those whose skill set complements yours. You will see your agency, influence, and satisfaction expand.

DETERMINATION

Ahmed Bukhash
Founder and chief architect, Archidentity, Dubai, and director of urban planning, Dubai Development Authority

→ Passion wins

Be passionate in your design abilities because many obstacles will come your way, some within your control and some not. Continue developing yourself through research and be attentive to your surroundings. Success will be achieved based on your perseverance.

Amr Amin
Senior design manager, Nine Yards Real Estate Development, United Arab Emirates

→ Don't underestimate yourself

If you don't really adore, respect, and admire architecture, then please find another career ASAP.

Human beings who will occupy buildings that may last for decades deserve an architect who works hard.

Never underestimate your capabilities. You can't imagine what you can really achieve.

Try new things. Explore the world and yourself.

Leila Sobek
Founder, BMA Studio, Dubai

→ Let passion be a catalyst

In the dynamic world of architecture, where the balance between creativity and practicality is an everyday challenge, the essence of success lies not only in planning and constructability but also in the underlying passion that drives you.

The architectural journey is evidence of the profound connection between the built environment and the human experience. Your passion for shaping spaces is what will distinguish you as an architect, setting you on a unique path where creativity and business can converge. If you let passion be the cornerstone of your practice, then clients cease to be mere patrons; they become collaborators in a shared vision. This empathetic connection results in designs that not only meet functional needs but also satisfy the human spirit.

Engaging with colleagues, contractors, and partners takes on a new dimension when passion leads the way. Collaborations become vibrant exchanges of ideas, fostering an environment where creativity flourishes.

Passionate architects go beyond the conventional boundaries of design, seamlessly integrating functionality with aesthetics. They push the limits, challenge norms, and create spaces that are timeless.

Passion is the catalyst that transforms an architectural practice into a thriving business. It drives architects to stay up on industry trends, embrace new technologies, and continually evolve.

When passion becomes the driving force, the business of architecture transcends mere transactions; it becomes a transformative journey that leaves a permanent mark on the built environment and the hearts of those it touches.

Mario Botta

Founder, Mario Botta Architetti, Mendrisio, Switzerland

→ Don't give up

Work, work, work.

Jesse Reiser and Nanako Umemoto
Founders, Reiser+Umemoto Architecture (RUR), New York

→ Defy the odds

There are a thousand reasons not to pursue architecture as an art, as a speculative cultural practice focused on building. The chances of being successful in the cultural domain of architecture are equivalent to those of making a stable living in the fine or performing arts. Despite these and other challenges, there are always some people willing to take the plunge. Three attributes are essential: talent, smarts, and will. Indomitable will. The ability to absorb setbacks, delays, and failure is critical. But when achievements come they are that much more rewarding, whether built or not. Good luck.

Thom Mayne

Founder, Morphosis, Los Angeles

→ Fall in love

Architecture is a long-term love affair. Were I to write a formula for it, I'd say it takes two parts optimism, one part obsession, a bit of denial, and a near-constant appreciation of the absurd. Luck, no doubt, plays a part as well. But the power of architecture comes from a commitment to an exhaustive exploration of a boundless territory that is not yet known or able to be conceptualized.

The requirement for optimism and determination conjures Lloyd Christmas's pursuit of a great beauty in *Dumb and Dumber*. "What are my chances of getting a date with you?" "A million to one," says she. Lighting the world with his smile, he replies, "Oh, so you're telling me I've got a chance!" Yup. That's architecture. The reality of the absurd? Well, that's the world we live in. It's the impact of chance on Chauncey Gardiner in *Being There*; it is *that* eccentric sometimes.

Relaxing into this reality will get you a very long way, especially if you go there amused while absolutely loving what you do every day. In short, you'll spend a lot of your time navigating a world that starts with "It's impossible" as you try to get to "Sounds interesting. Let's do it."

Are you addicted to solving for an uncountable multiplicity of inputs with constraints to most of them? Good. Does your brain go to a calm and clear place as it pushes forward to create something that was never conceptualized or understood before? Good. Is this absolutely what you must do? Better. Architecture is often more about who you are than what you do.

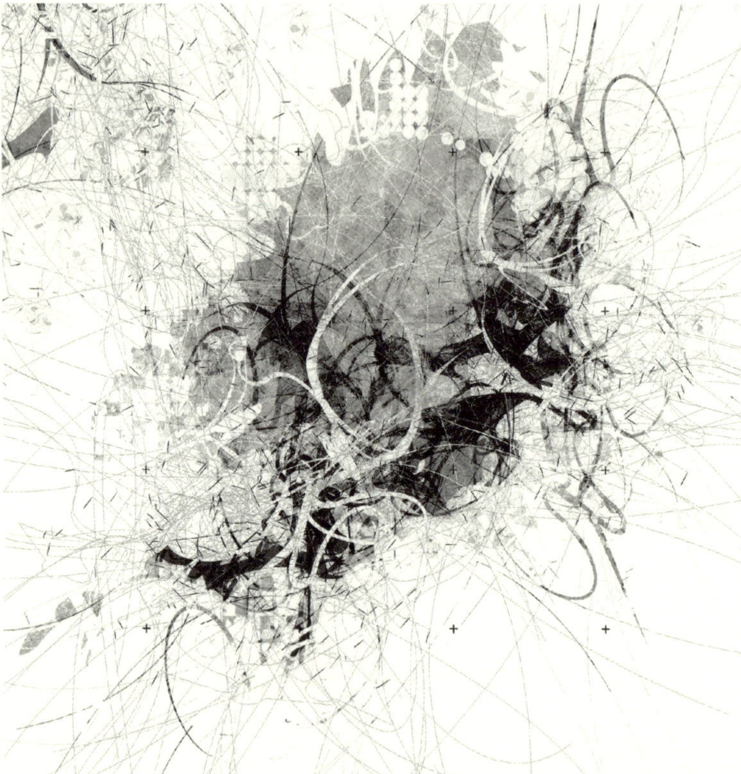

XCD_RURBAN by Thom Mayne

About the Authors

Raghda AlHayali is a millennial architect who started her professional journey in Dubai and is currently based in Canada. She is a graduate with honors from Ajman University, holding a bachelor of science in architectural engineering. Outside the realm of blueprints and steel, she unleashes her creativity through the written word. This passion has been her faithful companion since age thirteen, when she started an online journal that was notable for its unique content and garnered attention from national newspapers and radio shows.

For AlHayali, the act of writing holds a parallel significance to the art of designing. She embraces the field of architecture as a medium to articulate ideas, translating concealed imagination into tangible designs that shape the world. She aspires not only to build structures but also to make a positive impact with an unwavering commitment to sculpt the future for architects and society as a whole.

Clifford Pearson is a writer and editor who covers architecture, urbanism, and culture. He is a contributing editor at *Architectural Record*, where he served as deputy editor-in-chief and senior editor for twenty-six years. From 2018 through 2020, he was the editorial director of Kohn Pedersen Fox, and from 2016 to 2018, he was the director of the University of Southern California's American Academy in China and a lecturer at the USC School of Architecture. →

He has extensive experience in Asia, having overseen *Record*'s coverage in that region and serving as editor-in-charge of its China edition, 2008–2013. He is the co-author, with A. Eugene Kohn, of *The World by Design* (2019), the author of *Indonesia: Design and Culture* (1998), and the editor of *Modern American Houses* (1998). In 2004 and 2006, he was the co-curator of the U.S. Pavilion at the Venice Architecture Biennale. Pearson holds a master's degree in architectural history from Columbia University and a bachelor's degree in urban studies from Cornell University. Since 2021, he has served as joint artistic director of the Village Trip, an annual festival celebrating arts and activism in Greenwich Village.

Ken Yeang is an architect and ecologist with a long history in sustainable design and is the executive director of T.R. Hamzah & Yeang, a firm based in Kuala Lumpur and London. His pioneering work began with his research at Cambridge University in 1971. During the past forty years, he has developed guiding principles and systems in architecture that advance ecological design. His mission is to save the planet by design, reverse climate breakdown, and achieve a net-zero energy and carbon-neutral future. These are present in his built work and writings (twelve-plus instructive books).

His architecture is characterized by verdant biotic constituents (greenery) that create habitats to enhance local biodiversity and become living, human-made ecosystems.

Yeang trained at the Architecture Association (London). His doctoral thesis for Cambridge University was published as *Designing with Nature* (1985). He is an honorary fellow of Wolfson College, Cambridge. Awards for his innovations and architecture include the Aga Khan Award, the Prince Claus Award, the UIA Auguste Perret Prize, the Architectural Society of China Liang Sicheng Award, the Malaysian government's Merdeka Award, and the Malaysia Institute of Architects Gold Medal. In recognition of his dedicated work on a nature-based architecture, the *Guardian* named him one of the fifty people who could save the planet.

Image Credits

Page 16: Klein Dytham architecture
Page 27: Arthur Andersson
Page 32: Dong Gong
Page 35: Turenscape
Page 55: Liu Thai Ker
Page 57: Rocco Yim
Page 61: ARO with Heintges, TriPyramid Structures, and Boston Valley Terra Cotta
Page 66: Vasil Dimitrov via iStock (top image); bee32 via iStock (bottom); collage created by Calvin Tsao
Page 74: Rasem Badran
Page 78: Studio Gang
Page 88: Richard Hassell
Page 91: Weiss/Manfredi
Page 92: © Pasi Toiviainen
Page 99: T. R. Hamzah & Yeang
Page 105: Hitoshi Abe
Page 108: Arthur Andersson
Page 111: Zhu Pei
Page 124: Richard Fenne
Page 138: Thom Mayne

PUBLISHED BY
Princeton Architectural Press
A division of Chronicle Books LLC
70 West 36th Street, New York, NY 10018
papress.com

Printed and bound in China
28 27 26 25 4 3 2 1 First edition

EDITOR: Jennifer Thompson
DESIGNER: Paul Wagner

Library of Congress Cataloging-in-Publication Data
Names: Pearson, Clifford, editor. | Yeang, Ken, 1948– editor. | AlHayali, Raghda, editor.
Title: Tips from the top : architects share their advice for success / edited by Clifford Pearson, Ken Yeang, and Raghda AlHayali.
Other titles: Tips from the top (Princeton Architectural Press)
Description: First edition. | New York, NY : Princeton Architectural Press, 2025. | Summary: "Advice about getting started as an architect from a broad range of renowned international architecture and design professionals"— Provided by publisher.
Identifiers: LCCN 2024036051 | ISBN 9781797229980 (hardcover) | ISBN 9781797229997 (ebook)
Subjects: LCSH: Architecture—Vocational guidance. | Architectural practice.
Classification: LCC NA1995 .T57 2025 | DDC 720.23—dc23/eng/20240814
LC record available at https://lccn.loc.gov/2024036051